11+ Practice Papers
Book 2

Verbal Reasoning
Multiple Choice

(Papers 5 – 8)

Madeline Guyon

For Natasha and Stephanie

ISBN 978-0-9556590-1-0

Published by PHI Education
15, Pimms Grove, High Wycombe, Buckinghamshire, HP13 7EE

Paper 5

In these questions, **one letter** can be moved from the first word to the second word, thereby making **two new words.**
The order of the other letters must not be changed and both new words must be correctly spelt.
Find the letter that moves and mark it on your answer sheet.

Example

blow plum

Answer

b (the two new words are **low** and **plumb)**

QUESTION 1

spill rice

QUESTION 2

pride hone

QUESTION 3

spent desert

QUESTION 4

mitre rack

QUESTION 5

usage pond

QUESTION 6

grind fan

QUESTION 7

grate time

QUESTION 8

grain all

Move on to the next question

For these questions, fit the **same letter** into **both sets of brackets** to complete the words in front of the brackets and begin the words after the brackets.
Find this letter and mark it on your answer sheet.

Example

mea [?] **oble**
pi [?] **ew**

Answer

n (the four words are mean, noble, pin and new)

QUESTION 9

car [?] lea
sou [?] ale

QUESTION 10

lam [?] ach
dun [?] ars

QUESTION 11

dea [?] avy
bea [?] ame

QUESTION 12

bon [?] ale
we [?] oubt

QUESTION 13

el [?] arate
bea [?] art

QUESTION 14

chas [?] ellow
spas [?] ace

QUESTION 15

lon [?] nat
han [?] narled

Move on to the next question

In these questions, letters stand for numbers.
Work out the answer to each sum, then find the letter with that value and mark it on your answer sheet.

Example

If A = 3, B= 6, C = 8, D = 1,
E = 2,
what is the answer to this sum written as a letter ?
D + E + A = (?)

Answer

B

QUESTION 16

If A = 24, B = 36, C = 8,
D = 48, E = 6,
what is the answer to this sum written as a letter ?
E x C - A = (?)

QUESTION 17

If A = 5, B = 100, C = 7,
D = 35, E = 20,
what is the answer to this sum written as a letter ?
B ÷ E x C = (?)

QUESTION 18

If A = 9, B = 36, C = 8,
D = 42, E = 7,
what is the answer to this sum written as a letter ?
C x A - B = (?)

QUESTION 19

If A = 25, B = 85, C = 3,
D = 10, E = 65,
what is the answer to this sum written as a letter ?
A x C + D = (?)

Move on to the next question

QUESTION 20

If A = 6, B = 3, C = 30,
D = 36, E = 18,
what is the answer to this sum written as a letter ?
E ÷ B x A = (?)

QUESTION 21

If A = 21, B = 63, C = 3,
D = 9, E = 7,
what is the answer to this sum written as a letter ?
B ÷ D x C = (?)

QUESTION 22

If A = 36, B = 4, C = 3,
D = 27, E = 9,
what is the answer to this sum written as a letter ?
D ÷ C x B = (?)

QUESTION 23

If A = 34, B = 16, C = 108,
D = 91, E = 51,
what is the answer to this sum written as a letter ?
C - D + A = (?)

Move on to the next question

In these sentences, a **four-letter** word is hidden between two words that are next to each other.
Find the **two words** that contain the hidden word and mark them on your answer sheet.

Example

Her friends all stayed for tea.

Answer

for tea (the hidden word is **fort**)

QUESTION 24

Alec hobbled across the uneven ground.

QUESTION 25

The teenager was left home alone.

QUESTION 26

Henry didn't want to stop eating.

QUESTION 27

Patch, give me your paw now!

QUESTION 28

The tired baby shut his eyes.

QUESTION 29

Make sure you take enough time.

QUESTION 30

Grandma said raw vegetables are best.

Move on to the next question

Read the following information, find the correct answer to the question and mark the answer on your answer sheet.

QUESTION 31

Three friends agreed to meet in a park at 10:00. Bertie lived the furthest away and it took him 30 minutes to get to the park. Peter and Sam lived nearer to the park and their journeys each took 10 minutes less than Bertie's. If Peter arrived at the park at 10:05, what time did he leave home ?

Move on to the next question

In these questions, three of the five words are related. Find the **two** words that **do not go** with these three and mark them on your answer sheet.

Example

shiny red blue
paint green

Answer

shiny paint

QUESTION 32

dwelling rent lodging
home occupier

QUESTION 33

honest truthful genius
genuine innocent

QUESTION 34

crate chest shirt
back carton

QUESTION 35

chief head principle
principal moral

QUESTION 36

boat vessel weaving
blood craft

QUESTION 37

memory splendid memorable
forget remarkable

QUESTION 38

watch spectator actor
observer onlooker

Move on to the next question

For these questions, join a word from the first group with a word from the second group to make a correctly spelt, new word. The word from the first group must always come first and the order of the letters must not be changed.
Mark both words on your answer sheet.

Example

(out up down)
(bite like law)

Answer

out law (the word is **outlaw**)

QUESTION 39

(arm be though)
(less our are)

QUESTION 40

(house dig bet)
(old it raid)

QUESTION 41

(both off feat)
(her your ring)

QUESTION 42

(feat bar at)
(less all tend)

QUESTION 43

(at cone clue)
(tick tempt lass)

QUESTION 44

(bar end tier)
(age racks gin)

QUESTION 45

(pan sent end)
(try in there)

Move on to the next question

In these sentences, **three consecutive letters** have been taken out of the word in capitals.
These three letters spell a proper word without changing their order.
The sentence that you make must make sense.
Mark the correct three-letter word on your answer sheet.

Example

He **SPED** on the wet floor.

Answer

LIP (the word in capitals is **SLIPPED**)

QUESTION 46

The Met Office displays weather forecasts on its WEBE.

QUESTION 47

The traffic warden was obliged to IS a parking ticket.

QUESTION 48

The rides at the FGROUND were breathtaking.

QUESTION 49

The class was asked to CRE its own fairy story.

QUESTION 50

The skull and crossbones flag was hoisted on the PIE ship.

QUESTION 51

The weather had been quite DRY for days.

QUESTION 52

His aunty remarked upon the amount that he had GN.

Move on to the next question

For these questions, find **two words**, one from each group, that are **closest in meaning**.
Mark both of these words on your answer sheet.

Example

(button boat pull)
(rope tug push)

Answer

pull tug

QUESTION 53

(congested vacant spacious)
(indigestion crowded area)

QUESTION 54

(face retreat condemn)
(head mask confront)

QUESTION 55

(leave attire socks)
(dress alone attempt)

QUESTION 56

(particle delicate special)
(particularly fragment common)

QUESTION 57

(poem recite forget)
(repeat text learn)

QUESTION 58

(considerable consider kind)
(total regard cruel)

QUESTION 59

(unjust poem alter)
(adjust law lyrics)

Move on to the next question

Read the following information, find the correct answer to the question and mark the answer on your answer sheet.

QUESTION 60

Every morning at 10:00, John would set his watch 5 minutes faster than the time shown on the town hall clock. One day, however, the town hall clock was running fifteen minutes slow. What time did John's watch indicate that day when the real time was 11:20 ?

A 11:00
B 11:10
C 11:15
D 11:30
E 11:40

A B C D E F G H I J K L M N O P Q R S T U V W X Y Z
The alphabet above is provided to help you with these questions.
Find the next pair of letters for each series and mark the correct answer on your answer sheet.

Example

BZ CY DX EW FV (?)

Answer

GU

QUESTION 61

MN KL IJ GH EF (?)

QUESTION 62

XT AR DP GN JL (?)

Move on to the next question

QUESTION 63

WI VK TM QO MQ (?)

QUESTION 64

PH SK RJ UM TL (?)

QUESTION 65

RG SJ UO XV BE (?)

QUESTION 66

SR YP DN HL KJ (?)

QUESTION 67

NE QB PC SZ RA (?)

In these questions, the three numbers in each group below are related in the same way.
The first two groups have been completed for you.
Find the rule that connects the numbers in the first two groups and then use this rule to find the missing number in the third group. Mark this number on your answer sheet.

Example

(5 [10] 2) (6 [24] 4)
(8 [?] 2)

Answer

16

QUESTION 68

(3 [8] 4) (4 [15] 5)
(5 [?] 6)

QUESTION 69

(5 [26] 8) (7 [30] 8)
(8 [?] 9)

QUESTION 70

(10 [38] 14) (12 [48] 18)
(16 [?] 12)

Move on to the next question

QUESTION 71

(22 [7] 13)   (33 [16] 15)
(91 [?] 17)

QUESTION 72

(38 [21] 19)   (61 [31] 32)
(77 [?] 33)

QUESTION 73

(2 [6] 4)   (13 [50] 4)
(17 [?] 3)

QUESTION 74

(24 [14] 6)   (36 [16] 6)
(63 [?] 9)

Move on to the next question

In these questions, there are four words and the codes for **three** of them are shown.
These codes are **not** written in the same order as the words and one of the codes is missing.

PEAL PALE REAP READ
6945 6947 7489

Work out the correct code for each word and then answer the following questions.
Mark the correct answers on your answer sheet.

QUESTION 75

Which word has the number code **7948** ?

QUESTION 76

What is the number code for the word **PARE** ?

QUESTION 77

What is the number code for the word **PEAR** ?

Again, work out the correct code for each word below and then answer the following questions.
Mark the correct answers on your answer sheet.

SALE LEAP SEAT LAST
3562 3641 4635

QUESTION 78

Which word has the number code **4561**?

QUESTION 79

Find the number code for the word
SEAL ?

QUESTION 80

Find the number code for the word
TALE ?

End of Test Paper

Paper 6

In these questions, **one letter** can be moved from the first word to the second word, thereby making **two new words**. The order of the other letters must not be changed and both new words must be correctly spelt.
Find the letter that moves and mark it on your answer sheet.

Example

blow plum

Answer

b (the two new words are **low** and **plumb)**

QUESTION 1

cold cot

QUESTION 2

prime bat

QUESTION 3

could sage

QUESTION 4

chair plan

QUESTION 5

strip pores

QUESTION 6

loose pen

QUESTION 7

poker band

QUESTION 8

slime bred

Move on to the next question

In these questions, letters stand for numbers.
Work out the answer to each sum, then find the letter with that value and mark it on your answer sheet.

Example

If A = 3, B= 6, C = 8, D = 1, E = 2,
what is the answer to this sum
written as a letter ?
D + E + A = (?)

Answer

B

QUESTION 9

If A = 22, B = 24, C = 9,
D = 12, E = 86,
what is the answer to this sum
written as a letter ?
C x D - E = (?)

QUESTION 10

If A = 8, B = 11, C = 132,
D = 88, E = 96,
what is the answer to this sum
written as a letter ?
C ÷ B x A = (?)

QUESTION 11

If A = 131, B = 24, C = 107,
D = 119, E = 36,
what is the answer to this sum
written as a letter ?
D + B - E = (?)

QUESTION 12

If A = 22, B = 5, C = 13,
D = 7, E = 3,
what is the answer to this sum
written as a letter ?
E x B + D = (?)

Move on to the next question

QUESTION 13

If A = 45, B = 9, C = 22,
D = 6, E = 30,
what is the answer to this sum written as a letter ?
A ÷ B x D = (?)

QUESTION 14

If A = 56, B = 41, C = 9,
D = 24, E = 55,
what is the answer to this sum written as a letter ?
D + B – C = (?)

QUESTION 15

If A = 96, B = 144, C = 8,
D = 12, E = 108,
what is the answer to this sum written as a letter ?
B ÷ D x C = (?)

In these sentences, a **four-letter** word is hidden between two words that are next to each other.
Find the **two words** that contain the hidden word and mark them on your answer sheet.

Example

Her friends all stayed for tea.

Answer

for tea (the hidden word is **fort**)

QUESTION 16

The window nearest the fireplace opens.

QUESTION 17

They all searched for hidden treasure.

Move on to the next question

QUESTION 18

Tourists visit London all year round.

QUESTION 19

Annabel painted her wooden chair yellow.

QUESTION 20

Lucy really wanted a cream cake.

QUESTION 21

Alan moved a chest of drawers.

QUESTION 22

The company paid everyone their money.

For these questions, find the two words, **one from each set of brackets,** that will complete the statement in the best way.
Mark both words on your answer sheet.

Example

Fish is to
(chips scales cod)
as **bird** is to
(feathers nest wing).

Answer

scales feathers

QUESTION 23

Advance is to
(retard progress difficult)
as **hinder** is to
(delay middle easy).

Move on to the next question

QUESTION 24

Nurture is to
(history natural care)
as **neglect** is to
(disregard foster artificial).

QUESTION 25

Gorge is to
(valley Cheddar devour)
as **fast** is to
(starve slow quickly).

QUESTION 26

Infect is to
(disease contaminate spider)
as **cure** is to
(heel heal symptoms).

QUESTION 27

Gaggle is to
(mumble goats geese)
as **shoal** is to
(sheep fish shout).

QUESTION 28

Avoid is to
(hole dislike shirk)
as **engage** is to
(commit marry adore).

QUESTION 29

Discharge is to
(battery emit exclude)
as **absorb** is to
(consume wet approve).

Move on to the next question

Read the following information, find the correct answer to the question and mark the answer on your answer sheet.

QUESTION 30

Three builders each had to build a wall made up of 240 bricks. Builder A started at 09:00 and laid bricks at a rate of 60 bricks per hour. Builder B started 2 hours earlier and laid bricks at half the rate of Builder A. Builder C started at 10:00 and laid bricks at the rate of 80 bricks per hour. Which of the following statements is true ?

A Builder A finished first.
B Builder B finished first.
C Builder C finished first.
D Builder A and Builder C finished at the same time.
E All three builders finished at the same time.

In these questions, three of the five words are related. Find the **two** words that do not go with these three and mark them on your answer sheet.

Example

shiny red blue paint green

Answer

shiny paint

QUESTION 31

contract heat expand
agreement deal

QUESTION 32

deposit money extract
withdraw remove

Move on to the next question

QUESTION 33

Paris Australia London
Tokyo Canada

QUESTION 34

knee arm bone
elbow ankle

QUESTION 35

repeatedly often rarely
frequently never

QUESTION 36

tricky concave easy
difficult complex

QUESTION 37

trout perch budgie
gill salmon

In these sentences, **three consecutive letters** have been taken out of the word in capitals.
These three letters spell a proper word without changing their order.
The sentence that you make must make sense.
Mark the correct three-letter word on your answer sheet.

Example

He **SPED** on the wet floor.

Answer

LIP (the word in capitals is **SLIPPED**)

QUESTION 38

The train was delayed for three MIES at the station.

QUESTION 39

The soldiers continued to MH throughout the night.

QUESTION 40

The SP hill was difficult to climb.

Move on to the next question

QUESTION 41

TREAG on the grass was prohibited in the park.

QUESTION 42

The pan was full of BING water.

QUESTION 43

Her FAVITE flowers are petunias.

QUESTION 44

The policeman attempted to apprehend the CINAL.

Read the following information, find the correct answer to the question and mark the answer on your answer sheet.

QUESTION 45

The Martin family were considering a holiday destination. Dad was looking for a resort that offered live entertainment, a crèche and a golf course. Mum wanted a sandy beach, a crèche and live entertainment. Amy wanted a sandy beach but also wanted an adventure club. Beth, her sister, was looking for a resort that offered a sandy beach and live entertainment.
Which of the following statements is true ?

A Everyone wanted live entertainment.
B Mum and Amy wanted an adventure club.
C Beth, Amy and Dad wanted a sandy beach.
D Both Dad and Beth wanted a golf course.
E Only Mum and Dad wanted a crèche.

Move on to the next question

For these questions, you must find the correct number that will complete the sum and mark it on your answer sheet.

Example

5 + 8 = 9 + (?)

Answer

4

QUESTION 46

12 x 8 - 9 = 10 x 11 - (?)

QUESTION 47

13 x 11 - 41 = 9 x 12 - (?)

QUESTION 48

13 + 15 - 7 = 39 - (?)

QUESTION 49

125 ÷ 5 x 2 = 100 ÷ (?)

QUESTION 50

42 ÷ 6 + 15 = 5 x 6 - (?)

QUESTION 51

48 + 9 - 32 = 7 x 4 - (?)

QUESTION 52

15 x 3 - 7 = 6 x 6 + (?)

Move on to the next question

In the questions below there are two pairs of words.
On your answer sheet there are five words.
Mark one word on your answer sheet that will go equally well with both pairs of words.

Example

(instruct teach)
(wagons coaches)

Answer

train

QUESTION 53

(eider feathers)
(descend lower)

QUESTION 54

(boat freight)
(shove intrude)

QUESTION 55

(awning screen)
(sight eyes)

QUESTION 56

(seed particle)
(texture pattern)

QUESTION 57

(protect guard)
(thinking consciousness)

QUESTION 58

(east Asia)
(position bearing)

QUESTION 59

(emptied finished)
(tired fatigued)

Move on to the next question

In these questions, the middle word of each group has been made using some of the letters from the outer two words. The three words in the second group should go together in the same way as the three in the first group.
Find the word that is missing for the second group and mark it on your answer sheet.

Example

(etch [late] alter)
(trip [?] actor)

Answer

cart

QUESTION 60

(rode [cord] dice)
(also [?] nape)

QUESTION 61

(spike [piece] cheap)
(adept [?] leach)

QUESTION 62

(tribal [belt] better)
(chosen [?] bandit)

QUESTION 63

(staple [table] battle)
(assail [?] anchor)

QUESTION 64

(until [twirl] write)
(visit [?] angle)

QUESTION 65

(bradawl [board] robot)
(albeit [?] attain)

QUESTION 66

(track [coat] stock)
(arose [?] behalf)

Move on to the next question

In each question, find the number that continues the series and mark it on your answer sheet.

Example

4 8 12 16 20 (?)

Answer

24

QUESTION 67

25 24 27 26 29 (?)

QUESTION 68

91 90 88 87 85 (?)

QUESTION 69

17 22 26 29 31 (?)

QUESTION 70

38 35 45 42 52 (?)

QUESTION 71

2 10 40 120 (?)

QUESTION 72

10 18 34 66 (?)

QUESTION 73

3 5 8 13 21 (?)

Move on to the next question

A B C D E F G H I J K L M N O P Q R S T U V W X Y Z

The alphabet above is provided to help you with these questions.
For these questions, work out a different code for each question.
Find the correct answer and mark it on your answer sheet.

Example

If the code for CLAW is DMBX,
what is the code for LAMB ?

Answer

MBNC

QUESTION 74

If the code for THISTLE is VJKUVNG,
what does FWUVDKP mean ?

QUESTION 75

If the code for CARPET is ZXOMBQ,
what does TFKALT mean ?

QUESTION 76

If the word CHASE in code is BFXOZ,
what is the code for PASTE ?

QUESTION 77

If QFLPSF is the code for REMOTE,
what is CONTROL in code ?

QUESTION 78

If COACH in code is XLZXS,
what is the code for LORRY ?

Move on to the next question

QUESTION 79

If the code for BEAST is CBBPU,
what does CBBRUV mean ?

QUESTION 80

If the code for BONNET is CMQJJN,
what is the code for HOOD ?

End of Test Paper

PAPER 5
MULTIPLE CHOICE ANSWER SHEET

Score ________

NAME: ______________________ DATE: ________

Mark your answers with a single line

Example	1.	2.	3.	4.	5.	6.	7.	8.
b	s	p	s	m	u	g	g	g
l	p	r	p	i	s	r	r	r
o	i	i	e	t	a	i	a	a
w	l	d	n	r	g	n	t	i
	l	e	t	e	e	d	e	n

Example	9.	10.	11.	12.	13.	14.	15.
d	d	e	r	e	b	e	d
n	e	b	n	g	t	m	e
h	p	p	m	a	m	b	g
e	r	a	d	n	k	t	s
t	b	s	f	d	n	s	a

Example	16.	17.	18.	19.	20.	21.	22.	23.
A	A	A	A	A	A	A	A	A
B	B	B	B	B	B	B	B	B
C	C	C	C	C	C	C	C	C
D	D	D	D	D	D	D	D	D
E	E	E	E	E	E	E	E	E

Example	24.	25.	26.
Her friends	Alec hobbled	The teenager	Henry didn't
friends all	hobbled across	teenager was	didn't want
all stayed	across the	was left	want to
stayed for	the uneven	left home	to stop
for tea.	uneven ground.	home alone.	stop eating.

27.	28.	29.	30.
Patch, give	The tired	Make sure	Grandma said
give me	tired baby	sure you	said raw
me your	baby shut	you take	raw vegetables
your paw	shut his	take enough	vegetables are
paw now !	his eyes.	enough time.	are best.

31.	Example	32.	33.	34.	35.
09:25	shiny	dwelling	honest	crate	chief
09:45	red	rent	truthful	chest	head
09:55	blue	lodging	genius	shirt	principle
10:25	paint	home	genuine	back	principal
10:45	green	occupier	innocent	carton	moral

36.	37.	38.
boat	memory	watch
vessel	splendid	spectator
weaving	memorable	actor
blood	forget	observer
craft	remarkable	onlooker

PLEASE GO TO THE NEXT PAGE

Example: out, up, down, bite, like, law

39. arm, be, though, less, our, are

40. house, dig, bet, old, it, raid

41. both, off, feat, her, your, ring

42. feat, bar, at, less, all, tend

43. at, cone, clue, tick, tempt, lass

44. bar, end, tier, age, racks, gin

45. pan, sent, end, try, in, there

Example: ALL, TOP, LIP, LOP, SIP

46. LET, SIT, SKY, THE, EAR

47. SUE, WIN, HOE, ASH, SEW

48. OUR, EAR, AIR, ARE, ATE

49. RAY, EAT, SAY, ORE, SHE

50. RUT, OLD, ROT, HIP, RAT

51. TOW, TON, WIN, WET, EAR

52. OAR, ROE, ROW, OWE, OWN

Example: button, boat, pull, rope, tug, push

53. congested, vacant, spacious, indigestion, crowded, area

54. face, retreat, condemn, head, mask, confront

55. leave, attire, socks, dress, alone, attempt

56. particle, delicate, special, particularly, fragment, common

57. poem, recite, forget, repeat, text, learn

58. considerable, consider, kind, total, regard, cruel

59. unjust, poem, alter, adjust, law, lyrics

60. A, B, C, D, E

Example: GG, UG, FV, GU, GT

61. DD, CD, CC, DE, CB

62. GJ, NJ, MK, MJ, MN

63. HS, IS, QS, IT, HT

64. UI, WI, VI, QO, WO

65. FP, HO, GO, FO, GP

66. MH, NH, HH, MG, NG

67. OX, SY, UU, UX, UY

Example: 10, 15, 18, 16, 4

68. 24, 25, 30, 35, 36

69. 30, 34, 38, 64, 72

70. 30, 40, 44, 54, 50

71. 62, 66, 72, 74, 82

72. 32, 36, 42, 44, 46

73. 12, 14, 22, 49, 51

74. 7, 17, 19, 27, 28

75. PEAL, PALE, REAP, READ, PARE

76. 7468, 6469, 7946, 7469, 7489

77. 6945, 6947, 7489, 7469, 7946

78. LAST, SALE, SEAT, SEAL, LEAP

79. 4635, 4563, 4666, 4535, 4641

80. 1634, 1563, 1365, 1566, 1635

END OF TEST PAPER 5

PAPER 6
MULTIPLE CHOICE ANSWER SHEET

Score ________

NAME: ______________________ DATE: ________

Mark your answers with a single line

Example	1.	2.	3.	4.	5.	6.	7.	8.
b	c	p	c	c	s	l	p	s
l	o	r	o	h	t	o	o	l
o	l	i	u	a	r	o	k	i
w	d	m	l	i	i	s	e	m
		e	d	r	p	e	r	e

Example	9.	10.	11.	12.	13.	14.	15.
A	A	A	A	A	A	A	A
B	B	B	B	B	B	B	B
C	C	C	C	C	C	C	C
D	D	D	D	D	D	D	D
E	E	E	E	E	E	E	E

Example	16.	17.	18.	19.
Her friends	The window	They all	Tourists visit	Annabel painted
friends all	window nearest	all searched	visit London	painted her
all stayed	nearest the	searched for	London all	her wooden
stayed for	the fireplace	for hidden	all year	wooden chair
for tea.	fireplace opens.	hidden treasure.	year round.	chair yellow.

20.	21.	22.
Lucy really	Alan moved	The company
really wanted	moved a	company paid
wanted a	a chest	paid everyone
a cream	chest of	everyone their
cream cake.	of drawers.	their money.

Example		23.		24.		25.	
chips	feathers	retard	delay	history	disregard	valley	starve
scales	nest	progress	middle	natural	foster	Cheddar	slow
cod	wing	difficult	easy	care	artificial	devour	quickly

26.		27.		28.		29.	
disease	heel	mumble	sheep	hole	commit	battery	consume
contaminate	heal	goats	fish	dislike	marry	emit	wet
spider	symptoms	geese	shout	shirk	adore	exclude	approve

30.	Example	31.	32.	33.	34.	35.
A	shiny	contract	deposit	Paris	knee	repeatedly
B	red	heat	money	Australia	arm	often
C	blue	expand	extract	London	bone	rarely
D	paint	agreement	withdraw	Tokyo	elbow	frequently
E	green	deal	remove	Canada	ankle	never

36.	37.
tricky	trout
concave	perch
easy	budgie
difficult	gill
complex	salmon

PLEASE GO TO THE NEXT PAGE

Example	38.	39.	40.	41.	42.	43.	44.
ALL	NOT	OAT	ORE	DIN	OWL	OUR	RUN
TOP	NOR	ARC	WAS	SAP	OLD	EAR	MEN
LIP (marked)	TAR	ARK	TEA	SIP	HUB	ERR	RIM
LOP	NUT	OWE	IRE	RED	OIL	LOW	MAN
SIP	NIT	ILL	TEE	TIN	TUB	WIT	BUG

45.	Example	46.	47.	48.	49.	50.	51.	52.
A	7	21	2	11	2	4	1	1
B	11	23	4	13	4	6	3	2
C	4 (marked)	24	6	15	5	8	5	5
D	2	33	8	18	10	10	9	6
E	9	34	10	21	12	15	11	7

Example	53.	54.	55.
educate	bed	enter	blind
train (marked)	beak	float	blink
tutor	drop	barge	television
truck	down	push	glasses
rail	under	ship	curtains

56.	57.	58.	59.
wood	lock	locate	removed
grain	security	west	entranced
plant	awake	rotate	exhausted
leather	brain	orient	weary
element	mind	compass	sleepy

Example	60.	61.	62.	63.	64.	65.	66.
carp	pane	taped	base	snarl	stain	table	able
trap	plan	dealt	nose	choir	saint	alibi	hoes
tort	open	delta	said	chain	least	taint	shoe
coat	soap	cheap	sand	sails	slang	bleat	slab
cart (marked)	slap	peach	bone	snail	veins	latin	rose

Example	67.	68.	69.	70.	71.	72.	73.
22	28	82	30	46	200	102	26
24 (marked)	29	83	32	48	240	110	30
26	30	84	33	49	260	124	31
28	31	85	34	55	300	130	32
30	32	86	35	62	480	196	34

Example	74.	75.	76.	77.
MBNC (marked)	HYAENAS	WINERY	QCVXJ	BPMUQPK
WEYT	HYBRIDS	WINDOW	OCVXJ	DNOSSNM
DLAS	DUSTMAN	WICKET	QYPPZ	DPMUQPK
ASFG	DUSTBIN	WINDER	OYVXJ	BNOSSNM
GHDS	HYDRATE	QUAKER	OYPPZ	BPOUSPM

78.	79.	80.
GLIIB	BEACON	GMRZ
OLIIB	BEADED	GQLH
GJMMT	BEAGLE	IQLH
OLMMT	BEAUTY	IMRZ
OJIIB	BEAKER	IMLH

END OF TEST PAPER 6

PAPER 8
MULTIPLE CHOICE ANSWER SHEET

Score ________

NAME: ______________________ DATE: ________

Mark your answers with a single line

Example: b l o w
1. s p i n e
2. s p e l l
3. r a i s e
4. c l o n e
5. r o u t e
6. f e a s t
7. y o w l

Example: Her friends / friends all / all stayed / stayed for / for tea. (marked: for tea.)

8. We said / said prayers / prayers in / in church / church today.

9. Chris left / left her / her handbag / handbag at / at home.

10. Fairgrounds never / never admit / admit children / children under / under five.

11. Travelling for / for most / most people / people is / is tedious.

12. This is / is for / for all / all the / the children.

13. We drove / drove near / near to / to the / the city.

14. They really / really tried / tried to / to improve / improve relationships.

Example: chips / scales / cod — feathers / nest / wing (marked: scales, feathers)

15. animals / birds / water — writing / vegetables / sheep

16. blood / centre / love — veins / edge / disdain

17. sinister / cool / new — old / boring / harmless

18. economical / dull / forty — colourful / wasteful / money

19. take / disagree / break — consent / below / repair

20. tie / cello / rope — drum / knot / chain

21. outgoing / more / party — enter / withdrawn / horizontal

---

22. A / B / C / D / E

Example: SR / RR / RS / QS / PQ (marked: RS)

23. NW / NX / NY / OX / OY

24. OI / NI / PI / NH / OH

25. ZA / ZB / ZX / VX / VW

26. JH / HI / JK / HJ / HK

27. ST / SU / TT / TU / TV

28. QY / XY / XZ / WY / WX

29. BZ / BQ / BM / BP / AO

Example: shiny / red / blue / paint / green (marked: shiny, paint)

30. drive / grasp / brakes / seize / clutch

31. chart / graph / chair / table / dinner

32. raisin / contemporary / current / permanent / modern

33. diary / appoint / elect / choose / minister

34. schedule / scheme / crafty / plan / naughty

35. fang / elephant / bite / tooth / tusk

36. whiskers / broom / bristles / razor / stubble

PLEASE GO TO THE NEXT PAGE

11+ Practice Papers – Book 2 - Verbal Reasoning – Paper 8 – Multiple Choice Answer Sheet

Example
out, up, down | bite, like, law

37.
forget, at, but | ten, tack, tyre

38.
put, think, flour | down, in, rid

39.
ice, bar, on | bar, row, cue

40.
be, sea, bee | fore, sure, for

41.
of, see, in | tent, shore, turn

42.
bat, bet, son | shine, ray, tar

43.
band, car, read | rock, age, rubber

Example	44.	45.	46.	47.	48.	49.	50.
ALL	ART	ROE	ARK	TAN	IMP	RIP	PAR
TOP	OAK	OWN	RAT	TAG	MET	FIR	ART
LIP	CAR	PUT	TIE	VAN	RIM	RAT	LAW
LOP	RUM	ONE	TEE	WON	EAT	FOR	ONE
SIP	RAM	ROW	TEA	ANT	IRE	PAR	OWN

51.	Example	52.	53.	54.	55.	56.	57.	58.
A	7	1	5	4	10	6	1	4
B	11	3	6	5	11	10	2	5
C	4	5	7	10	12	12	3	6
D	2	6	8	15	13	18	4	7
E	9	7	9	17	14	20	5	8

Example	59.	60.	61.	62.	63.	64.	65.
GG	KW	RW	LT	ST	JO	IA	ZV
UG	JV	SX	OW	RT	LO	GY	YV
FV	JX	SV	OT	RR	JQ	HZ	LV
GU	LV	SC	LW	QT	LQ	IZ	MV
GT	KX	SW	OS	QR	LP	HA	NV

Example	66.	67.	68.	69.	70.	71.	72.	73.
14	29	71	7	26	0	31	51	45
16	31	73	17	30	2	37	59	54
26	39	79	18	32	4	41	64	59
10	49	81	42	34	18	47	67	69
6	52	83	52	40	20	51	69	76

Example	74.	75.	76.	77.
MBNC	SHAME	FIGMENT	PXJBY	KOGQR
WEYT	SHINE	FICTION	PYJBY	KQGUR
DLAS	RHINO	GADGETS	PYLEC	OQKUV
ASFG	RHYME	XEROXES	TCPIG	OMKQV
GHDS	RANGE	FABRICS	TDRLL	KOGUR

78.	79.	80.
FGCNGT	RELATE	ATAAKD
FHCOGU	SIMPLE	JGQXGK
BHYOCU	SERIES	CSEXQY
ABZIBO	SERIAL	AWYFGK
FBCIGO	RESCUE	AWZDJG

END OF TEST PAPER 8

Paper 7

In these questions, **one letter** can be moved from the first word to the second word, thereby making **two new words.**
The order of the other letters must not be changed and both new words must be correctly spelt.
Find the letter that moves and mark it on your answer sheet.

Example

blow   plum

Answer

b (the two new words are **low** and **plumb)**

QUESTION 1

strap   good

QUESTION 2

grave   shot

QUESTION 3

brake   coal

QUESTION 4

trace   due

QUESTION 5

arise   place

QUESTION 6

print   tone

QUESTION 7

slant   tone

QUESTION 8

frank   alter

Move on to the next question

For these questions, fit the **same letter** into **both sets of brackets** to complete the words in front of the brackets and begin the words after the brackets.
Find this letter and mark it on your answer sheet.

Example

mea [?] **oble**
pi [?] **ew**

Answer

n (The four words are mean, noble, pin, new.)

QUESTION 9

plum [?] ats
dau [?] ase

QUESTION 10

foo [?] ads
cur [?] ady

QUESTION 11

face [?] eas
stou [?] eak

QUESTION 12

crou [?] eas
cha [?] ace

QUESTION 13

bea [?] one
cla [?] aive

QUESTION 14

hur [?] eak
bai [?] oud

QUESTION 15

mil [?] art
blan [?] aft

Move on to the next question

In these questions, letters stand for numbers. Work out the answer to each sum, then find its letter and mark on the answer sheet.

Example

If $A = 3, B = 6, C = 8, D = 1, E = 2$,
what is the answer to this sum written as a letter ?
$D + E + A = (\ ?\ )$

Answer

B

QUESTION 16

If $A = 39, B = 3, C = 2, D = 26, E = 56$,
what is the answer to this sum written as a letter ?
$A \div B \times C = (\ ?\ )$

QUESTION 17

If $A = 14, B = 12, C = 19, D = 21, E = 16$,
what is the answer to this sum written as a letter ?
$E + C - D = (\ ?\ )$

QUESTION 18

If $A = 62, B = 12, C = 6, D = 8, E = 24$,
what is the answer to this sum written as a letter ?
$D \times D + C - A = (\ ?\ )$

QUESTION 19

If $A = 8, B = 0, C = 4, D = 22, E = 12$,
what is the answer to this sum written as a letter ?
$B \times A + E = (\ ?\ )$

Move on to the next question

QUESTION 20

If $A = 4, B = 2, C = 24, D = 10, E = 20$,
what is the answer to this sum written as a letter ?
$D \div B \times A = (\ ?\ )$

QUESTION 21

If $A = 41, B = 97, C = 4, D = 45, E = 56$,
what is the answer to this sum written as a letter ?
$B - E + C = (\ ?\ )$

QUESTION 22

If $A = 25, B = 9, C = 48, D = 2, E = 7$,
what is the answer to this sum written as a letter ?
$A \times D + E - B = (\ ?\ )$

In these sentences, a **four-letter** word is hidden between two words that are next to each other.
Find the **two words** that contain the hidden word and mark them on your answer sheet.

Example

Her friends all stayed for tea.

Answer

for tea (the hidden word is **fort**)

QUESTION 23

The protestors are angry with developments.

QUESTION 24

Julie regularly attended a riding school.

Move on to the next question

QUESTION 25

We had green peas every day.

QUESTION 26

Elle chose the green Wellington boots.

QUESTION 27

The small boat created gentle ripples.

QUESTION 28

They crawled along the same ditch.

QUESTION 29

We said each was just fine.

Read the following information, find the correct answer to the question and mark the answer on your answer sheet.

QUESTION 30

Whilst Alex only had half as many marbles as Brian, he had 3 more than Charlie. His friend Donald had five more than Charlie. If Donald has 8 marbles, how many marbles did Brian have ?

A 3
B 6
C 8
D 12
E 14

Move on to the next question

In these questions, three of the five words are related. Find the **two** words that do **not** go with these three and mark them on your answer sheet.

Example

shiny red blue paint green

Answer

shiny paint

QUESTION 31

plan outline design
pen ruler

QUESTION 32

partition wall bricks
floor screen

QUESTION 33

path root pedestrian
route passsage

QUESTION 34

anxious cry difficult
uneasy worried

QUESTION 35

fawn boots kit
adult kid

QUESTION 36

red shade umbrella
tint hue

QUESTION 37

detached terrace verandah
barbeque patio

Move on to the next question

In these sentences, **three consecutive letters** have been taken out of the word in capitals.
These three letters spell a proper word without changing their order.
The sentence that you make must make sense.
Mark the correct three-letter word on your answer sheet.

Example

He **SPED** on the wet floor.

Answer

LIP (the word in capitals is **SLIPPED**)

QUESTION 38

Rain clouds were GARING in the sky.

QUESTION 39

The squirrel lay DORT throughout the winter.

QUESTION 40

The cold ice cream hurt her SENIVE teeth.

QUESTION 41

The papers were fed through the SHDER.

QUESTION 42

He was cultivating his TOOES in the greenhouse.

QUESTION 43

He put the CH on the table.

QUESTION 44

The student conducted much of his RERCH in the library.

Move on to the next question

For these questions, find **two words**, one from each group, that are **closest in meaning**.
Mark both of these words on your answer sheet.

Example

(button boat pull)
(rope tug push)

Answer

pull tug

QUESTION 45

(calculate deteriorate bad)
(worsen improve speculate)

QUESTION 46

(aversion attraction detour)
(road holiday diversion)

QUESTION 47

(answer ignorance ignore)
(question response puzzle)

QUESTION 48

(burn discourage reprimand)
(quench scold encourage)

QUESTION 49

(hesitate battery play)
(charge pause work)

QUESTION 50

(motive innocent guilty)
(emotive reason blame)

QUESTION 51

(infirm educate ignore)
(listen class inform)

Move on to the next question

Below are two groups of words. Choose **two words**, one from each group, that are most **opposite** in meaning.
Mark the two words on your answer sheet.

Example

(garden in shop)
(up hotel out)

Answer

in out

QUESTION 52

(amicable aggressive joke)
(comical hostile laugh)

QUESTION 53

(lively passive energetic)
(overtake active small)

QUESTION 54

(telescope shorten brief)
(abbreviate condense extend)

QUESTION 55

(puncture clock punctual)
(timely appointment late)

QUESTION 56

(awesome boastful impression)
(amazing unimpressive mould)

QUESTION 57

(formal accident dinner)
(official casual dress)

QUESTION 58

(vulgar domestic civil)
(rude engineer criminal)

Move on to the next question

Read the following information, find the correct answer to the question and mark the answer on your answer sheet.

QUESTION 59

Glyn replaces the rear tyres on his car 3,000 miles and those on the front every 4,000 miles. If all four tyres were changed when the car had covered 12,000 miles, at what mileage will he again change all four tyres at the same time ?

A 15,000 miles
B 16,000 miles
C 18,000 miles
D 21,000 miles
E 24,000 miles

In these questions, there are three pairs of words in brackets.
The second word, in each of the first two brackets, has been formed using some of the letters from the first word.
Find the missing word in the third bracket in the same way as the first two brackets.
Mark the correct answer on your answer sheet.

Example

(piglet pet) (driven den)
(astute [?])

Answer

ate

QUESTION 60

(feast seat) (falter tale)
(falsely [?])

QUESTION 61

(pastels sap) (generals leg)
(sabotaged [?])

Move on to the next question

QUESTION 62

(ballet able) (amateur mate)
(apples [?])

QUESTION 63

(spinster sine) (goalkeeper gale)
(peasants [?])

QUESTION 64

(reaper pear) (leaping peal)
(leasing [?])

QUESTION 65

(apparatus pat) (undoing dog)
(defining [?])

QUESTION 66

(retracting tear) (hillside dish)
(nephews [?])

QUESTION 67

(camp damp) (ball call)
(fate [?])

Move on to the next question

In these questions, there are four words and the codes for **three** of them are shown.
These codes are **not** written in the same order as the words and one of the codes is missing.

SOUL LOUD SUMO LOOP
8445 2468 2634

Work out the correct code for each word and then answer the following questions.
Mark the correct answers on your answer sheet.

QUESTION 68

Which word has the number code **8445** ?

QUESTION 69

Find the number code for the word **POOL.**

QUESTION 70

Find the number code for the word **LOOM.**

Again, work out the correct code for each word below and then answer the following questions.
Mark the correct answers on your answer sheet.

POET DOME NOSE DOES
1357 6359 6325

QUESTION 71

Which word has the number code **6325** ?

QUESTION 72

Find the number code for the word **POEM.**

QUESTION 73

Find the number code for the word **TOES.**

Move on to the next question

In each question, find the number that continues the series in the most sensible way and mark it on the answer sheet.

Example

4 8 12 16 20 (?)

Answer

24

QUESTION 74

42 45 48 51 (?)

QUESTION 75

40 46 51 55 (?)

QUESTION 76

26 29 27 30 28 (?)

31 ✓

QUESTION 77

1 2 4 8 (?)

QUESTION 78

21 23 15 19 9 15 (?)

QUESTION 79

61 36 56 37 51 38 (?)

QUESTION 80

3 7 15 31 63 (?)

End of Test Paper

Paper 8

In these questions, **one letter** can be moved from the first word to the second word, thereby making **two new words.**
The order of the other letters must not be changed and both new words must be correctly spelt.
Find the letter that moves and mark it on your answer sheet.

Example

blow plum

Answer

b (the two new words are **low** and **plumb)**

QUESTION 1

spine super

QUESTION 2

spell urge

QUESTION 3

raise loud

QUESTION 4

clone fee

QUESTION 5

route clod

QUESTION 6

feast ample

QUESTION 7

yowl dirt

Move on to the next question

In these sentences, a **four-letter** word is hidden between two words that are next to each other.
Find the **two words** that contain the hidden word and mark them on your answer sheet.

Example

Her friends all stayed for tea.

Answer

for tea (the hidden word is **fort**)

QUESTION 8

We said prayers in church today.

QUESTION 9

Chris left her handbag at home.

QUESTION 10

Fairgrounds never
admit children under five.

QUESTION 11

Travelling for most people is
tedious.

QUESTION 12

This is for all the children.

QUESTION 13

We drove near to the city.

QUESTION 14

They really tried to
improve relationships.

Move on to the next question

For these questions, find the two words, **one from each set of brackets**, that will complete the statement in the best way.
Mark both words on your answer sheet.

Example

Fish is to
(chips scales cod)
as **bird** is to
(feathers nest wing).

Answer

scales feathers

QUESTION 15

Aviary is to
(animals birds water)
as pen is to
(writing vegetables sheep).

QUESTION 16

Heart is to
(blood centre love)
as perimeter is to
(veins edge disdain).

QUESTION 17

Wicked is to
(sinister cool new)
as innocuous is to
(old boring harmless).

QUESTION 18

Thrifty is to
(economical dull forty)
as extravagant is to
(colourful wasteful money).

Move on to the next question

QUESTION 19

Challenge is to
(take disagree break)
as submit is to
(consent below repair).

QUESTION 20

String is to
(tie cello rope)
as percussion is to
(drum knot chain).

QUESTION 21

Extrovert is to
(outgoing more party)
as introvert is to
(enter withdrawn horizontal).

Move on to the next question

Read the following information, find the correct answer to the question and mark the answer on your answer sheet.

QUESTION 22

In a high-rise tower block, George lives 8 floors above Cassie and three floors below Jessica. Jessica lives on the 13th floor. If Sammy lives one floor below Cassie, on which floor does he live ?

A The 1st floor.
B The 2nd floor.
C The 5th floor.
D The 8th floor.
E The 12th floor.

Move on to the next question

A B C D E F G H I J K L M N O P Q R S T U V W X Y Z
The alphabet above is provided to help you with these questions.
For these questions, find the letters that complete the statement in the best way and mark the answer on your answer sheet.

Example

CD is to **EF**
as **PQ** is to (?).

Answer

RS

QUESTION 23

PL is to **SO**
as **KU** is to (?).

QUESTION 24

RG is to **JM**
as **WC** is to (?).

QUESTION 25

QS is to **OQ**
as **XY** is to (?).

QUESTION 26

HG is to **KK**
as **EF** is to (?).

QUESTION 27

DE is to **LK**
as **LN** is to (?).

QUESTION 28

GC is to **TX**
as **DB** is to (?).

QUESTION 29

AM is to **AZ**
as **BD** is to (?).

Move on to the next question

In these questions, three of the five words are related. Find the **two** words that do **not** go with these three and mark them on your answer sheet.

Example

shiny red blue
paint green

Answer

shiny paint

QUESTION 30

drive grasp brakes
seize clutch

QUESTION 31

chart graph chair
table dinner

QUESTION 32

raisin contemporary current
permanent modern

QUESTION 33

diary appoint elect
choose minister

QUESTION 34

schedule scheme crafty
plan naughty

QUESTION 35

fang elephant bite
tooth tusk

QUESTION 36

whiskers broom bristles
razor stubble

Move on to the next question

For these questions, join a word from the first group with a word from the second group to make a correctly spelt, new word. The word from the first group must always come first and the order of the letters must not be changed.
Mark both words on your answer sheet.

Example

(out up down)
(bite like law)

Answer

out law (the word is **outlaw**)

QUESTION 37

(forget at but)
(ten tack tyre)

QUESTION 38

(put think flour)
(down in rid)

QUESTION 39

(ice bar on)
(bar row cue)

QUESTION 40

(be sea bee)
(fore sure for)

QUESTION 41

(of see in)
(tent shore turn)

QUESTION 42

(bat bet son)
(shine ray tar)

QUESTION 43

(band car read)
(rock age rubber)

Move on to the next question

In these sentences, **three consecutive letters** have been taken out of the word in capitals.
These three letters spell a proper word without changing their order.
The sentence that you make must make sense.
Mark the correct three-letter word on your answer sheet.

Example

He **SPED** on the wet floor.

Answer

LIP (the word in capitals is **SLIPPED**)

QUESTION 44

They were **STLED** by the clap of thunder.

QUESTION 45

The clothes were **THN** into an untidy pile.

QUESTION 46

Amy and Leanne enjoy going to **PARS**.

QUESTION 47

The local football team had the **ADTAGE** in the second half.

QUESTION 48

They planted trees around the **PERIER** of the plot.

QUESTION 49

The liquid leaked out of the **PERATIONS**.

QUESTION 50

Nowadays there are concerns regarding the holes in the **OZ** layer.

Move on to the next question

Read the following information, find the correct answer to the question and mark the answer on your answer sheet.

QUESTION 51

Henry the dog has 2 meals a day. His friend Sheba eats half as often. Their friend Tyza eats twice as often as Sheba but each of his meals is half the size of those given to both Henry and Sheba.

Which of the following statements is true ?

A All 3 dogs eat the same amount each day.
B Sheba eats the least in a day.
C Henry and Tyza each eat more than Sheba.
D Henry eats the most.
E Tyza eats the least.

For these questions, you must find the correct number that will complete the sum and mark it on your answer sheet.

Example

5 + 8 = 9 + (?)

Answer

4

QUESTION 52

28 ÷ 7 x 8 = 100 ÷ 4 + (?)

QUESTION 53

175 ÷ 25 x 6 = 7 x (?)

QUESTION 54

121 ÷ 11 x 5 + 7 = 9 x 8 – (?)

QUESTION 55

33 + 75 + 9 = 9 x (?)

Move on to the next question

QUESTION 56

4 x 8 - 20 = 6 x 3 - (?)

QUESTION 57

72 ÷ 9 + 7 = 4 x 5 - (?)

QUESTION 58

7 x 6 + 7 = 55 - (?)

ABCDEFGHIJKLMNOPQRSTUVWXYZ

The alphabet above is provided to help you with these questions.
Find the next pair of letters for each series and mark the correct answer on your answer sheet.

Example

BZ CY DX EW FV (?)

Answer

GU

QUESTION 59

AM CO EQ GS IU (?)

QUESTION 60

DL GI JF MC PZ (?)

QUESTION 61

QR WO ZI FF IZ (?)

QUESTION 62

KK IN FS BZ WI (?)

QUESTION 63

ZA XC TG RI NM (?)

QUESTION 64

BY ZV WR SM NG (?)

QUESTION 65

HA KZ GY LX FW (?)

Move on to the next question

In these questions, the three numbers in each group below are related in the same way.
The first two groups have been completed for you.
Find the rule that connects the numbers in the first two groups and then use this rule to find the missing number in the third group. Mark this number on your answer sheet.

Example

(5 [10] 2) (6 [24] 4)
(8 [?] 2)

Answer

16

QUESTION 66

(7 [42] 6) (9 [63] 7)
(3 [?] 13)

QUESTION 67

(12 [20] 10) (18 [35] 19)
(44 [?] 37)

QUESTION 68

(68 [14] 17) (76 [14] 19)
(49 [?] 7)

QUESTION 69

(4 [30] 13) (9 [39] 15)
(4 [?] 18)

QUESTION 70

(61 [54] 5) (17 [7] 8)
(12 [?] 10)

QUESTION 71

(30 [17] 15) (46 [31] 17)
(53 [?] 14)

QUESTION 72

(5 [35] 8) (6 [37] 7)
(8 [?] 8)

QUESTION 73

(39 [91] 13) (27 [63] 9)
(31 [?] 7)

Move on to the next question

ABCDEFGHIJKLMNOPQRSTUVWXYZ
The alphabet above is provided to help you with these questions.
For these questions, work out a different code for each question.
Find the correct answer and mark it on your answer sheet.

Example

If the code for CLAW is DMBX,
what is the code for LAMB ?

Answer
MBNC

QUESTION 74

If the code for REASON is UHDVRQ,
what does UKBPH mean ?

QUESTION 75

If the code for SCIENCE is OYEAJYA,
what does BEYPEKJ mean ?

QUESTION 76

If the word CHOICE in code is AEKDWX,
what is the code for RANGE ?

QUESTION 77

If UCRGP is the code for WATER,
what is MOIST in code ?

QUESTION 78

If the code for CHEQUE is EEGNWB,
what is the code for DEALER ?

Move on to the next question

QUESTION 79

If the code for TIMBER is GRNYVI,
what does HVIRVH mean ?

QUESTION 80

If the code for KETTLE is JGQXGK,
what is the code for BUBBLE ?

End of Test Paper

Answers

Paper 5

1	p	41	feat her
2	p	42	at tend
3	s	43	at tempt
4	t	44	bar racks
5	u	45	pan try
6	g	46	SIT
7	r	47	SUE
8	g	48	AIR
9	p	49	EAT
10	e	50	RAT
11	n	51	EAR
12	d	52	ROW
13	k	53	congested crowded
14	m	54	face confront
15	g	55	attire dress
16	A	56	particle fragment
17	D	57	recite repeat
18	B	58	consider regard
19	B	59	alter adjust
20	D	60	B
21	A	61	CD
22	A	62	MJ
23	E	63	HS
24	Alec hobbled	64	WO
25	home alone.	65	GP
26	stop eating	66	MH
27	paw now !	67	UX
28	shut his	68	24
29	take enough	69	34
30	said raw	70	40
31	09:45	71	72
32	rent occupier	72	46
33	genius innocent	73	49
34	shirt back	74	17
35	principle moral	75	PEAL
36	weaving blood	76	7469
37	memory forget	77	7946
38	watch actor	78	SEAT
39	arm our	79	4563
40	dig it	80	1635

Paper 6

1	l	41	DIN
2	e	42	OIL
3	u	43	OUR
4	i	44	RIM
5	s	45	E
6	o	46	23
7	r	47	6
8	e	48	18
9	A	49	2
10	E	50	8
11	C	51	3
12	A	52	2
13	E	53	down
14	A	54	barge
15	A	55	blind
16	window nearest	56	grain
17	hidden treasure	57	mind
18	all year	58	orient
19	chair yellow	59	exhausted
20	a cream	60	plan
21	a chest	61	dealt
22	paid everyone	62	sand
23	progress delay	63	snail
24	care disregard	64	saint
25	devour starve	65	table
26	contaminate heal	66	shoe
27	geese fish	67	28
28	shirk commit	68	84
29	emit consume	69	32
30	D	70	49
31	heat expand	71	240
32	deposit money	72	130
33	Australia Canada	73	34
34	arm bone	74	DUSTBIN
35	rarely never	75	WINDOW
36	concave easy	76	OYPPZ
37	budgie gill	77	BPMUQPK
38	NUT	78	OLIIB
39	ARC	79	BEAUTY
40	TEE	80	IMRZ

Answers

Paper 7

1	s	41	RED
2	r	42	MAT
3	r	43	LOT
4	t	44	SEA
5	a	45	deteriorate worsen
6	r	46	detour diversion
7	n	47	answer response
8	f	48	reprimand scold
9	b	49	hesitate pause
10	l	50	motive reason
11	t	51	educate inform
12	p	52	amicable hostile
13	n	53	passive active
14	l	54	shorten extend
15	d	55	punctual late
16	D	56	awesome unimpressive
17	A	57	formal casual
18	D	58	civil rude
19	E	59	E
20	E	60	sale
21	D	61	gas
22	C	62	pale
23	are angry	63	past
24	a riding	64	seal
25	peas every	65	fin
26	Elle chose	66	seen
27	created gentle	67	gate
28	same ditch	68	LOOP
29	said each	69	5448
30	D	70	8443
31	pen ruler	71	DOME
32	bricks floor	72	1352
33	root pedestrian	73	7359
34	cry difficult	74	54
35	boots adult	75	58
36	red umbrella	76	31
37	detached barbeque	77	16
38	THE	78	3
39	MAN	79	46
40	SIT	80	127

Paper 8

1	p	41	in tent
2	p	42	bet ray
3	a	43	band age
4	l	44	ART
5	u	45	ROW
6	s	46	TIE
7	y	47	VAN
8	in church	48	MET
9	Chris left	49	FOR
10	admit children	50	ONE
11	for most	51	D
12	for all	52	7
13	drove near	53	6
14	improve relationships	54	10
15	birds sheep	55	13
16	centre edge	56	6
17	sinister harmless	57	5
18	economical wasteful	58	6
19	disagree consent	59	KW
20	cello drum	60	SW
21	outgoing withdrawn	61	OW
22	A	62	QT
23	NX	63	LO
24	OI	64	HZ
25	VW	65	MV
26	HJ	66	39
27	TT	67	79
28	WY	68	17
29	BQ	69	40
30	drive brakes	70	0
31	chair dinner	71	41
32	raisin permanent	72	59
33	diary minister	73	69
34	crafty naughty	74	RHYME
35	elephant bite	75	FICTION
36	broom razor	76	PXJBY
37	at tack	77	KQGUR
38	put rid	78	FBCIGO
39	bar row	79	SERIES
40	be fore	80	AWYFGK